After a vivid dream warning me that we are in jeopardy because of our many years of dishonoring Mother Earth and the despair of trees and plants, I was inspired to write this poetic journey from the heart. This book is woven with verses that resonate with the wisdom of ancient trees through the whispers of nature's soul by the words of a beautiful, tiny, illuminated insect.

I was in awe of this tiny flying creature who spoke so eloquently, yet with talks of a dire warning. It's time we heed the plea of the trees, the guardians of our green sanctuary, and teach our children to be stewards of this fragile world. The trees consume what we create, and we breathe what the trees exhale. This book is a call to action, an anthem for change, and a testament to the enduring power of Mother Earth.

May this book remind us that we are not alone in this intricate vibration of existence and that by embracing the wisdom of Mother Nature and nurturing a profound connection with the Earth, we can forge a brighter, more sustainable future for the next seven generations.

This book belongs to

For my husband Victor and children, George, Annalyse, Adam, Sean, Marcus, Alex, and Victor II, and my grandchildren, Anastaysia, Nataliya, Jenavieve, Caius, and Atlas

The Whispering Vibrations of Nature

A poem

Tyrese Gould Jacinto
Art by Arnild C. Aldepolla

Amid winds breath, flow gentle leaves,

Moving slightly by her sweet, blowing breeze,

We hear her warning and vibrational song,

Whispered by trees of the forest, we belong.

For years, we've lived with no concern or care,

With reckless blindness, now we must bear,

With our greed, wants, and desires, we caused,

The trees and plants to rise to a call.

The trees, they vibrate in a silent rampage,

Their roots suckling at the spoil of soil,

They see us and know our time is near,

We sealed our fate in the hands of our toil.

The streams that once flowed pure and clear,

Now, carry our waste of contaminated tears,

And the air we breathe, once clear and clean,

Now filled with poisonous breath as we breathe.

The forest, it knows us now, as it waits,

For we continue down this path of fate,

For it knows that one day we'll destroy us all,

For our lack of care and to hear the call.

And that day, that moment, is nearing us all,

We're forced to face the wrath, vibration, the call.

We'll remember the vibrational warning we hear,

We'll know that we've chosen the path we feared.

Let us hear the forest's wrestling vibrational call,

Take heed of the poisonous air, water, and soil,

We have come to realize, and now have learned,

The forest will destroy us, and we will be the soil.

Watching the rustling leaves of the soaring trees,

Is our only warning that the forest doeth breathe,

We have silenced the vibrations of hearts from within,

We do not listen to the earth's cries; we shall not win.

Time has ended, poisoning the air we breathe,

The forest retaliates with its wilted leaves,

The once great vibration for us now fades away,

And amongst the trees is no longer a place to play.

We are one with the water that flows with life,

Now, water struggles with contamination by no right,

And the trees and plants know we're to blame,

Creatures that thrived watch us all with shame.

We are one with the soil that nurtures our life,

And is poisoned by carelessness and without strife,

The trees and plants mourn the loss of what is dear,

As we continue to destroy it year after year.

The forest is living and hears the vibration of hearts,

It knows the damage that we think we are apart,

It vibrates with the harm that we have brought,

Vibrations that warned us, but we heard naught.

For if we do find a common healing sound,

The trees and plants will reclaim their place,

And we will bear witness to their power,

As they find it necessary to restore their flower.

We see what the trees and plants have warned,

They vibrate and strive as they have mourned,

For only together can we hope to find,

A way to save the destruction we have left behind.

We hear the symphony of trees and plants,

Harmonious orchestra for all to dance,

A vibration where every leaf, petal, and stem,

Living, breathing, being like us, not apart from them.

The trees and plants that we vibrate with,

Are dancing and swaying with the whisper of the wind,

They are a chorus, a choir of beings that hum,

A sentiment of life that we all have become.

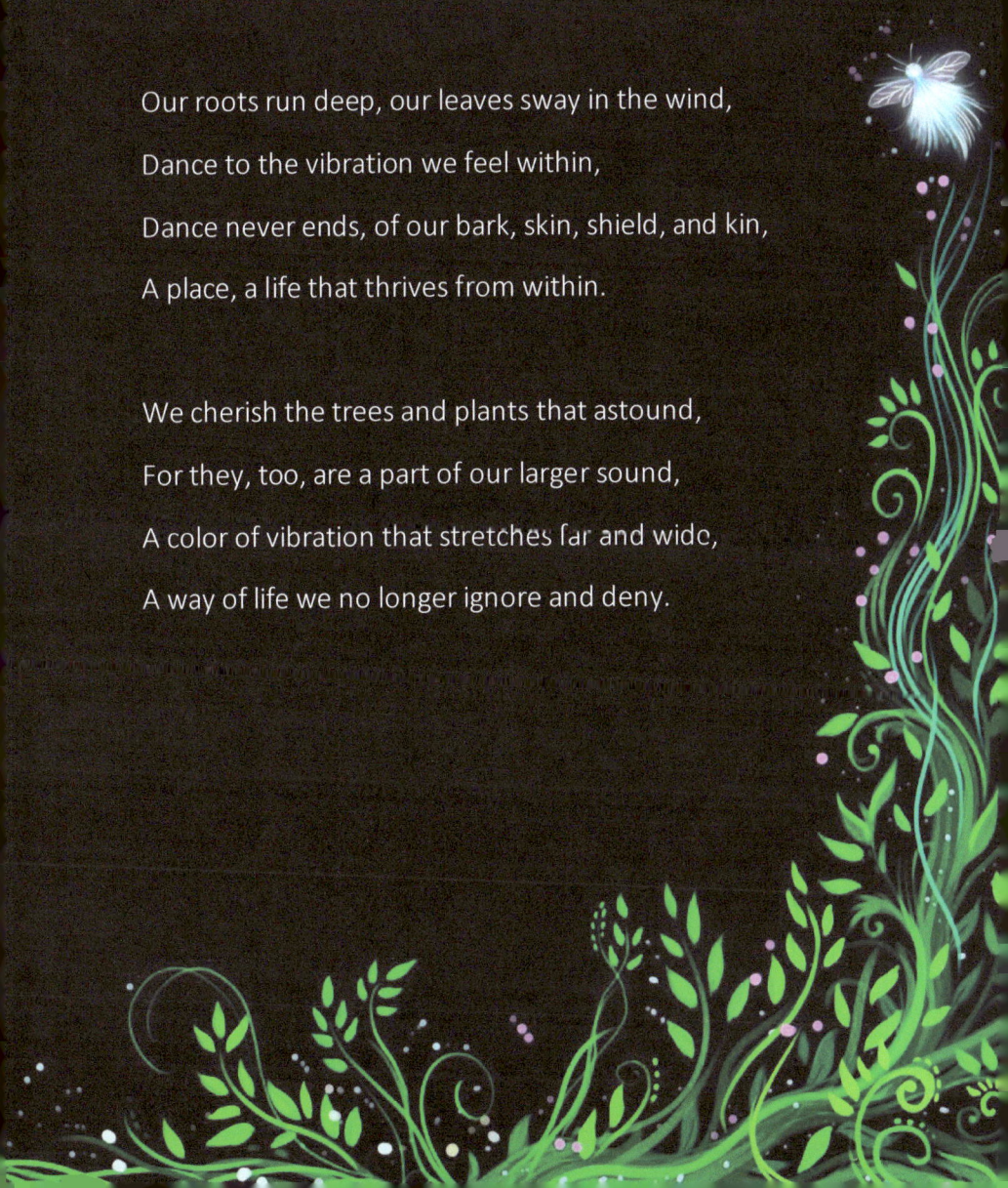

Our roots run deep, our leaves sway in the wind,

Dance to the vibration we feel within,

Dance never ends, of our bark, skin, shield, and kin,

A place, a life that thrives from within.

We cherish the trees and plants that astound,

For they, too, are a part of our larger sound,

A color of vibration that stretches far and wide,

A way of life we no longer ignore and deny.

Colonization has silenced the song from within,

With concrete jungles, where nature cannot begin,

With blinding the beauty that surrounds us all,

Forgotten the wisdom of her sounds and the call.

We listen closely, we hear the whisperers' sounds,

Vibrations of leaves, hum of trees, the songs of the flowers,

The wisdom they share, history and the stories of despair,

Of life, of love, of growth, and of nature's own cares.

We are in tune with the vibrations all around,

To the songs of life that are often not found,

For in our silence lies a universe of sounds,

Of living, breathing, and vibrating all that bounds.

For we, as humans, have often been taught,

That we are the rulers, but we are the ones at fault,

No dominance over Mother Earth, or mastery of life,

But the spite of our arrogance, we lost the fight.

Trees and plants, gifts of nature, a great force,

Much greater than us, a power we cannot source,

Vibration, the beginning, ending, and all in between,

We cannot conquer, no matter how hard we scheme.

Mountains crash upon us, the ocean waves roar,

Trees whisper secrets, the skies too vast to explore,

Animals roam free, and plants grow wild,

We, only humans, a mere part of nature's brief smile.

One with nature, a mere part of her plan,

A cog in the wheel, only a single strand,

We are not rulers but merely guests,

Allowed to live, to learn, to love, and to rest.

Trees and plants give, and nature takes away,

Nature holds a balance in her own mysterious way,

We are only humans; we have yet to learn,

We can only borrow; we do not deserve to earn.

Feel the vibration of power, of the trees and plants,

Listen to its songs of wisdom as we fall into a trance,

In the end, it is nature, she will live and thrive,

We, as merely humans, without her, cannot survive.

Walk within the forest, amongst the trees and plants,

Vibrate with wisdom, that comes with this chance,

We are not alone; we vibrate the song of life,

Every breath we take is only a borrowed entice.

Swaying trees above us and plants we walk within,

Remind us of vibrations and our songs, as we begin,

Life is a gift for us, the blessings have begun,

Every living being, now reverenced with true love.

Live one with nature, one with the trees and plants,

Healing from destruction as we hear her sweet chants,

Listen to lessons of nature, mysteries that she holds,

Walk with reverence amongst them, never too bold.

All the steps we take, leave a vibration behind,

A mark on Mother Nature, can never be untwined,

Every word we utter, every vibration we designed,

Is a ripple effect on trees, plants never to unbind.

As we start to vibrate, with nature all around,

Of life that thrives and the beauty it astounds,

Let us remember, we are all guests here,

Borrowing each place, our step has ever seared.

As the end is nearing, it is not that which we take,

But that which we give, that truly makes us great,

Let us walk with respect, every step with care,

Leave alone our nature, and we vibrate with care.

As we learn to live one with the trees and plants,

Remember, we are guests, as a passing glance,

The steps left behind and the breath we breathe,

Borrowed from nature, we now respect and believe.

Find your hidden sanctuary, in trees and plants,

Sacred space, a place, a life thrives at its own pace.

We, only humans, must tread lightly as we walk,

Impacts on Mother Nature's, vibration and thought.

The trees flow above us, plants at our feet bloom,

For us to be as one, to vibrate in our earthly room,

They are a part of us, and we part of them,

A tapestry of songs that bind as we all blend.

Every tree that falls, every plant we uproot,

Lasting ripple effects, that runs through the root,

The earth, air, water, the vastness of the sky,

A lasting chain reaction, we cannot ignore or deny.

Vibrate amongst the trees, plants with respect,

Cherish every moment of our every little step,

As we remember, we humans are merely guests,

Nature's mighty power will surely concur the best.

Mother Nature, she reminds us, she gives all life,

Her majestic duty, to vibrate with all her might,

A legacy, seven generations, that are to come,

A world where nature thrives, we vibrate, as one.

We become silent and take heed of our fears,

Heed the warnings of trees, plants that are here,

They vibrate a simple song, not for our ears,

Our hearts feel the warning, a vibration we can feel.

Forest, plants, and trees that vibrate all around,

Singing a sweet song, a vibration so profound,

As time is short, waking on a path of destruction,

Nature's wrath wins, now no more instruction.

We hear vibrations, sounds in the darkness,

Only a small segment of this incredible vastness,

Of this larger picture, of life and of fate,

We must vibrate together before it's too late.

As we vibrate on the road of carelessness,

Face the consequence of utter helplessness,

Nature will demolish with her power and might,

We will face a world with no chance in sight.

Now heed the warning, vibrate with trees and plants,

Stop greed and taking before nature takes a stance,

Vibrate sounds in harmony with nature all around,

Protect Mother with all might, as we are bound.

The end is here; vibration and song we preserve,

Heeding the sounds of nature, we listen, observe,

To trees, plants, seven generations of our Creator,

A new song, a new sound we hear the

Whispering Vibrations of Nature.